How to Recognize and Overcome Victim Mentality

DONNA LIVELY

How to Recognize and Overcome Victim Mentality

DONNA LIVELY

http://www.donnalively.com

DONNA LIVELY

ISBN:1475230362
ISBN-13:9781475230369

DEDICATION

This book is for all my friends and family
Who listened to my stories, and thought I have a story
which needs to be told.

DONNA LIVELY

ACKNOWLEDGMENTS

To all of my family and lifelong friends, old and new, I am happy to share my path with all of you. Thank you for your set of eyes and insights.

Thanks to my husband Brett who tolerates my idiosyncrasies without judging.

Thanks to my daughter, son and granddaughter for believing in me.

To quote Buddha: What we think, we become. All that we are arises with our thoughts. With our thoughts, we make the world.

DONNA LIVELY

CONTENTS

DONNA LIVELY

1

INTRODUCTION

We all get to sit and cry; we all get to wonder why. We all get to experience pain; we all have days we cannot explain.

This is an excellent way to describe the human condition. Regardless of the level of intensity everybody has the blues sometimes, and there is not a lot of choice in the matter. However, there is a choice we do manage to make; it is whether or not we're going to live as victims or victors.

I've tried to understand what goes into the victim mentality which seems to be so prevalent these days.

A victim mentality is a constant and global mindset which says: *I am what I am because of unfair treatment by an individual, group or system, and, I cannot rise above it. Therefore, I am not RESPONSIBLE for my actions I am the victim.* This is a mini version of the victim mentality, and I think we can all identify with it.

In order to be healthy, we have to incorporate a strong, mind, body and spirit. Let's examine how we can get one step towards health with eliminating the victim mentality we may be experiencing.

[i] I want to make a clear distinction between someone treating us as a victim and having a victim mentality. It is not like the old horse and carriage; we can have one without the other. Abusers to feel victimized by the people they are hurting emotionally or even physically are a typical scenario. On the other hand, we may be genuinely victimized by someone and still not think or act like a victim.

Raised in the typical suburban home; with a mother, father, and five siblings, (all girls), I am the third of six. I had difficultly taking responsibility from a young age, for situations I envisioned did not go my way. I remember one scene in particular; my older sister Dianne's friend allowed me to borrow an

encyclopedia from her collection. I was in the

eighth grade and had to complete a report for school, so because my parents did not own encyclopedias, I borrowed Bonnie's.

What happened taught me to return borrowed items immediately.

From the age of five until I was nineteen, I lived in a split-level house, which from time, to time, flooded with both surface water and raw sewage. My parents had this house built after coming upon the land; it was their dream to create a home, for at the time, their four girls.

I admit now, as a child, I did not keep my bedroom neat and tidy. This infuriated my younger sister Darlene since we shared the room. To this day she maintains an impeccable bedroom and home!

After completing the piece I used the encyclopedia for, I did not immediately return it. Before I had the opportunity to, during a severe rain storm, the house flooded. My bedroom, located on the lower level, flooded this night. The encyclopedia on my bedroom floor, amongst everything else I chose to *hang* on the floor, was ruined by the raw sewage.

My mother, in her clamoring, familiar voice, ordered me to call Bonnie and tell her what happened. It was not my fault the house flooded and ruined her book. Why should I have to tell her? I am the victim here!

See how we make ourselves into the victim?

Weeks later, I worked up the guts to tell Bonnie what happened to her book she confidently lent me. Of course, I did not tell the whole truth about what happened; the fact I am a *slob* and a *pig* (my mother's pet names for me), and left her book on my bedroom floor!

Bonnie understood and was not too worried because this particular edition was from an older set, and she had a newer, updated one.

At one time or another, everyone becomes the victim, but the question is, are we truly the victim?

I remember the emotions I experienced when the encyclopedia became ruined; anger, fear and a victim of circumstance. In reality, I was not the victim in this situation.

2

CHANGING THE SELF IN
SELF-ESTEEM

When judging an experience as unfair or a
tragedy, we automatically experience anger,
emotional withdrawal, depression, anxiety or
other painful emotions which support the
notion of you or another as a victim.

Here, is a question to ponder:

How much could we strengthen self-esteem, happiness,

and creative productivity if we were never in a victim mindset?

Everyone desires a healthy level of self-esteem, but few seem to know how to get it.

Self-esteem is how we feel about ourselves not how others feel about us. We trust believe and experience ourselves as worthy people. We think we deserve to be happy.

[ii] All successful people in society understand their egos are an asset. Top performers in athletics, business, or any other profession are convinced they can be heroes, and it shows.

Our response to all aspects of life is shaped by self-concept and self-esteem. It is the most powerful judgment we make about ourselves.

Self-esteem consists of one's feelings about personal competence, ability to cope with life, personal worth, ones right to be happy, ones right to stand up for ourselves, our interests, needs, and worthiness to live life and be productive members of society. It is the reputation we acquire with ourselves.

There is nothing wrong with being proud of what we've done, or what we think we can do, or from where we came.

The higher your self-esteem, the more we love ourselves, the better we get along with others, and, the more we accomplish.

Margaret Thatcher once said, ***"I wasn't lucky I deserve it"***. *Pride is necessary to improve our current situation.*

Just as, individuals present behaviors typical of their character type when they are experiencing positive self-esteem, they exhibit a different personality type when they are experiencing low self-esteem. Low self-esteem is often the cause of adverse behaviors, which, lead to poor performance and low productivity.

How do we build self-esteem?

Most people increase their self-esteem by d*oing*. They take action over and over again.

When evaluating your self-image, reference all your success instead of failures (even though there are almost always more failures).

Look for new and significant challenges. Look to learn more and open new horizons. Building confidence is the result of taking tough actions and emphasizing your successes.

It is the most difficult task which instills a sense of accomplishment and builds confidence. If the challenge is strong enough, even failing can leave you with the positive attitude, as long as you gave it your best shot.

When I married young, I suffered low self-esteem. I married one of the first guys I dated. My parents did not allow their daughters to date until we were sixteen. My belief at the time was if I did not marry this guy I would become a spinster. Why was my self-esteem low?

I blamed everyone and everything in my life, which never got me anywhere. I was like a puppy chasing its tail!

Then one day I discovered low self-esteem is often at the heart of one's emotional struggle. For many years, I struggled with many emotional issues. I now realize I brought almost all of the issues to myself. I went to several psychologists throughout the years, and I now know a deeper understanding of myself, a higher level of awareness, and new ways to live a more meaningful, happier life is possible through therapy. [iii]

Over the years, I've learned a *victim mentality* is unhealthy, regardless of whether one is a victim of trauma, or unfortunate circumstances. This mentality leads to blaming others, which does not improve one's emotional well-being. Through therapy, I learned everyone needs to be heard, understood, accepted, and validated.

One defines therapy in many ways. Find

what is comfortable. Whether it is
professional treatment, support groups,
friends and family support, or any other form
of *positive therapy*, learn what works for you.
Do not be afraid to engage in more than one
kind, the more the merrier!

A Change of Attitude

In May 1992, after seven years of
experiencing multiple symptoms the diagnosis
is readmitting, reoccurring Multiple Sclerosis.
Images of what- could be flashed through my
mind. Here, I was, thirty-three years old, a
marriage of thirteen years, two children, ages
six and eleven, and this news devastated me.
The once smiling, carefree gal I worked hard
to be, was now sporting a mouth which
sagged into a frown by default. Many months
after the diagnosis, I was through feeling like a

victim and knew the only way to modify these feelings was to change my attitude. I was spending too much time feeling sorry for myself because of all the things I could not do anymore.

I made a conscience decision, focus on the things I could do! I accepted I would no longer be able to do some of the physical activities I enjoyed, but realized the essence of me had not changed. I am still the same caring, creative person I had always been. I still have something to give my family and the world.

Taking Action

Knowing it was time to take action; I sat down with a pen and paper and honestly evaluated my priorities. Much to my surprise, most of what precious energy I had, I expended on things not high on my priorities list. I was doing what I thought I had to or "should" do while the things which were most dear to me, I ignored or postponed.

It Is Up To YOU

Whether you are a victim or a victor, is a matter of choice. No one has to be a victim. You can take control of your attitude, actions, healthcare, and life. You can choose to be a victor.

CHANGE IS POSSIBLE

Change is inevitable it is a process, and it is not a quick fix. Change requires time, effort, courage, awareness, openness, determination, persistence and faith.

Change comes with time, and with the use of therapy-it is an unfolding, evolving, and goal-oriented approach to healing. It occurs when you work through your pain and find your inner strength, leading you on a journey of self-growth and development.

Change in behavior, thought, emotion, perspective, and coping skills are the ultimate goal. Therapy can help you face the pain and let you to develop new and appropriate goals.

Always remember your power!

Make several copies of the following paragraph and put them where you will read them aloud throughout your day. Hang one on the bathroom mirror, your office cubical, and refrigerator. Repeat it and *believe* it, and watch the change!

I have a tremendous amount of power to: ask for support, face fears, be kind to myself, forgive myself, and be thankful for

what I have. I can and will create healthy
relationships, live in the moment, express
feelings, and see my blocks. I can and will
manage my thoughts, let go of resentment
and anger, create positive change, and
cultivate happiness.

DONNA LIVELY

3

HOW TO STOP VICTIM MENTALITY THINKING IN CHILDREN

[iv] *"It's not my fault. That is not fair!"*

How many times has your child clamored this when upset? Although it is often difficult to know how to respond to this as a parent, know it is common for children and teens to feel this way from time to time.

Children have acute "fairness descry" than we do because their perspective is still relatively immature. If the child holds onto this feeling of unjustness, he or she will begin to feel like a victim. The danger comes in when your child holds onto this feeling of injustice all the time, and begins to feel like a victim. When this happens, the parent will see the child begin to use this stance to manipulate people and get what they want.

When a child feels like a victim, they will begin to *act* like a victim. They will begin to conceive because something they think is not fair, the rules do not apply to them.

This pattern of Unfairness-Victim Stance-Manipulation often starts at home; parents unwittingly play into it. Sadly, the behavior *can* move to other areas of your child's life. If your ten-year-old thinks you aren't being fair, it often then becomes, "My teacher is not fair; school is not fair my coach is not fair." If unchecked, this mindset can extend into the teen years and eventually into your child's adult life and will turn into a chronic state of mind. You will hear, "My boss is not fair," or "It's my spouse's fault." Remember, fairness detectors become keener as we play into them. We teach kids to be victims and to whine—and to become complaining, whining adults.

If you would like more information about what you as a parent can do to stop this cycle, visit her site at:

http://www.empoweringparents.com/How-to-Stop-Victim-Mentality-Thinking-ids.php#

I believe it is necessary to prevent victim mentality in children before they turn into whining teens and adults.

4

ZEN THINKING ABOUT VICTIM MENTALITY

Life will continually teach us lessons. If one fails to learn these lessons then life will keep repeating them, a winner learns by experience. A victim refuses to learn, keeps doing the same things and keeps receiving the same outcomes.

ᵛDo you have Victim Mentality? Not sure? Answer the following:

Do you say or think, any or all of these statements on a regular basis?

"It's not my fault!"

"I did not have the time, or I do not have the time"!

"I am not a lucky person".

If you are likely to uttering the above phrases or even thinking them, you are putting yourself in the role of the victim. This is the language a victim uses. What the victim seeks to do is to shift blame. They shovel blame off onto everybody but themselves. A person using this language is not seeking to learn from his or her experiences.

Ask, yourself the following:

Why do you think it is not your fault?

Why didn't I have the time?

Why am I not lucky?

Why don't you ever get what you deserve?

There is an extremely easy answer to all of these maladies.

You probably will not like it; in fact I know you will not.

HERE, IT IS:

You do not want to take responsibility for outcomes because it is much easier to shift blame.

Anybody who ever achieved anything took responsibility for the outcome. You may not win the first time, or the next, or the third, or even the tenth time. You might not even win the fiftieth time! Colonel Sanders did not. Neither did Thomas Edison.

Today we can all eat Kentucky Fried Chicken (*for health reasons I do not*) under an electric light (if we so desire!)

The point is— every time you fail you understand what does not work. What does this allow you to do? It allows you to reload, refocus then move in another direction. Only a fool keeps doing the same thing over and over again expecting a different outcome. It is like watching the same movie over and over again anticipating a different ending. This formula has never worked and never will work. This is what victims do.

5

"RESPONSIBILITY IS THE PRICE OF GREATNESS"

Winston Churchill

I believe you do not consider yourself a fool,
yet you could be sabotaging yourself by
succumbing to victim mentality.

Life will continually teach us lessons. If we fail to learn these lessons then life will keep repeating them.   When we keep making excuses for ourselves instead of seeking

solutions, we will always take on the role of a victim.

A victim mentality can be overcome. Keep trying. This is all it takes. Find better ways to do things, learn. We can turn victim mentality into champion mentality. All it takes is a willingness to learn and some discipline to keep trying.

We slip easily into victim mentality when we try to get exactly what we want in less than ideal circumstances, and when we cannot, we allow ourselves to be trapped in no-win choices. Often, we are not even willing to consider any choice other than the ideal choice. When we are in victim mentality, we do not see the collection of choices we have, and we wallow in resentment. We feel helpless.

In order to eliminate our victim mentality, we must:

A. Start accepting the reality of the situation instead of trying to achieve the ideal.

B. Find the best option available within the reality of the circumstances, and then:

C. Accept the choice, instead of resenting it.

These examples show how to consider various circumstances/relationships:

vi **Victim Mind-Set Example**

I want to meet up with my friend for coffee, and she is chronically late. I may feel as the victim by choosing between having to wait, and not getting to see her. I wait and then feel disconnected and irritated.

Empowered Mind-Set Example

I do not want to feel like a victim. I have many choices. I can accept my friend is always late and chose to:

A. Be late too

B. Take a terrific book and have 15 minutes of quiet time

C. Meet near a place where I need to run errands and let her know I will wait ten minutes and if she is not there, I'll leave

D. Meet her at my house so I can keep doing whatever I want till she gets there and if she does not arrive before my next appointment, she will not **get** to see me

Your choice is to take control of your situation; you have no reason to feel like a victim.

Victim Mind-Set Example:

My husband and I will be invited to my parents for Easter Dinner. All my family will be attending. I want to attend, my husband does not. This situation could issue an argument— if you allow it.

    A. You can choose to argue with your husband, even try to make him feel guilty for not wanting to attend

    B. You can demand he attends and threaten him by assuring you will not have sex with him

    C. He agrees to attend, and the whole time you are at the event, he wears a frown and makes you feel uncomfortable because you know you insisted he attend and now you are both miserable.

Empowered Mind-Set Example:

Why let your blood pressure rise and allow yourself to be angry?

A. Your spouse is aware of the invitation. IF he chooses to attend and plans to enjoy himself, great

B. If he chooses NOT to attend, this is also notable. By him not attending, you may attend the function, enjoy yourself and see his decision was correct, not only for himself, but you. You both did what each of you wanted. I guess this is a win-win.

C. R-E-S-P-E-C-T, We must respect each other and one another's adult decision

The world is not an ideal place. When we look for ideal choices and model solutions, we find we have fewer and fewer choices'. We think like victims, which usually involves feeling both helpless and angry.

If we know we are making choices in situations which are not ideal and accept this, then we will suddenly see countless choices previously invisible to us. We will experience greater freedom and take more responsibility for the choices we do make. Doing so, we can dramatically alter how we feel about ourselves and the level of intimacy we have with others.

When married to my first husband, for a long time I felt like a victim. It took me time, and therapy to look at situations in a different way. Now I know I was not a victim. We all have choices, and because I was *afraid* to make choices I knew I wanted, it was not his fault. I had to take responsibility and make a choice. I chose to ask him for a divorce after 20 years of marriage and two children.

I remember talking to one of my psychologists and complaining about different things. All of the sentences started with *he should have* or *she should have*. I'll never forget what my psychologist asked me. She looked straight at me and asked "Who wrote the book of *should.*

Wow, she had me! It was ME who thought everyone should do things the way I wanted it done!!!

This was a tremendous eye opener for me, and I think a decisive turn in my therapy. I had to stop blaming others and accept responsibility!

I hope this has helped gain insight about how

to become increasingly empowered even in

circumstances which are less than idea.

6

ARE YOU LIVING WITH A VICTIM MENTALITY?

Here, is a quiz to help determine if you are carrying around victim mentality, which may be robbing you of your sense of personal power. Answer True or False to the following statements: [vii]

A. My first reaction to a setback is to blame someone else for what's happened.

B   No matter what I do, things are not going to change for me.

C   I often find myself to be beginning thoughts with phrases like "I cannot…", "I'm no good at…". "I've never been able to…"

D   When things go wrong, I tend to beat myself up.

E   Sometimes I'm lucky, but when things happen they are because I mess up.

F   When angry, I rarely begin sentences with "I".

G   Conversations with friends are usually about how hard my life is.

H   When friends offer advice, I usually answer it with a "Yes, but…"   since

they cannot know how difficult my
situation is

I   I spend a fair amount of my time
thinking about past failures and mistakes.

J   Other people usually cause me to feel
the way I do. I would be more centered if
it were not for them.

K   I'm always so busy with work and the
things I need to do to survive, I just do not
have time to do things I want to do for
myself.

L   I'd like to exercise more and eat in a
healthier way, but I just cannot right now.

M   If I was not tied down to so many
obligations, I could do some of the things
I always think about doing.

N   Someday I'll find a new partner who
will change my life. In the meantime, hope.

O   I must have done something horrible

in a past life because nothing I do ever work out.

P   If only I had more support, I could have… (Fill in the blank)

Add up your score. The higher your score, more likely you are to think of yourself as a victim.

From a young age, victimhood is usually a way of staying stuck in old patterns and can be an externalizing way of dealing with unacknowledged anger or fear of change.

If you have answered true to more than five of these questions, chances are you would benefit from a closer look at what's happening in your life right now.

7

WHY TAKING RESPONSIBILITY IS THE MOST IMPORTANT STEP TO YOUR HEALTH AND WELL-BEING

People who often shirk responsibility often fall into victim mentality. It is everyone's fault they are not happy (not getting a promotion, not succeeding in their marriage, etc.) —except their own.

There will be times when things are not your fault, and you may even be thinking of some of those times right now.

Taking responsibility does not mean you are always at fault, only you acknowledge your part and let it go (meaning you do not perpetually blame others.) [viii]

Those who have succumbed to the victim mentality, however, often exhibit the following characteristics:

A. You think you are unlucky, and there is nothing you can do about it

B. You think you are pretty much always right

C. You rarely, if ever, apologize

D. You often feel sorry for yourself

E. You believe if others are acting badly,

you can also (I.e., If Bob comes in late for work every day, then so can I.)

Did you notice these characteristics are surrounded by negativity? In fact, people who do not accept responsibility are often harboring this negativity in them—in the form of sadness, hopelessness, anger, depression, anxiety, fear, guilt, insecurity and a host of other negative emotions.

Over time, and even in the short-term, holding on to such negative thoughts can lead to chronic stress and, from there, chronic disease.

Are you ready to take responsibility? Let's start by defining what the word responsibility is. This is how the Merriam-Webster Dictionary defines it:

re·spon·si·bil·i·ty

1: the quality or state of

being   : as

A: moral, legal, or mental

accountability

2: something for which

one is   : <has

neglected his

responsibilities>

The great thing about taking responsibility
is it opens the door to anything you want.
You get to choose what in your life you want
to stay and what should go. How do you get
to this point? It is pretty straightforward.
Begin by letting go of the negative emotions
and self-limiting beliefs which are causing you
to be stuck in a victim mentality.

The best part is, once you *feel* you are in
charge (instead of a victim), you will *act* like

you are in charge, and your life will act
accordingly. You will also find you can easily

adopt the following positive traits of people,
who take responsibility, including:

a. Accepting when you are wrong and
apologizing

B. Asking others for help when you need
it

C. Having empathy for others

D. Admitting when you have made a
mistake

E. Forgiving others easily

F. Being open-minded to the opinions of
others

G. Believing your life is meant to be
great

Once you let go of self-sabotaging beliefs and behaviors, your life will be limitless in the happiness, health and wellbeing it will create for you and those around you.

My diagnosis of multiple sclerosis is what changed my way of thinking. When I learned living negative would have a negative impact on my path with the disease, I had to make decisions for myself.

For once in my life, I had to think about **ME** first! I knew in order to get healthy and stay healthy I had to change my attitude, my surroundings and people in my life. I could no longer be around negative people I must remain positive and have positive in my life. It was not too many years after my diagnosis I made the decision to leave my husband. I needed positive energy surrounding me, something I did not have. It was time for a

CHANGE, and I did it! I'm not saying it was easy, change can be scary.

8

THE VICTIM ATTITUDE

CHOOSING HOW TO SPEAK

Our society has a *victim culture* in which many
tend to avoid taking responsibility, yet they
blame others and say or think, *poor me.* This is
reflected in the news, media and songs, as well
as in language. [ix]

Be aware of the way you think, talk and how it may indicate a victim mentality. The following are examples of what victim mentality may sound like:

Look at what you made me do

It is not my fault

Can you believe what she did to me?

It is not fair

I don't have enough time

My boss does not respect me

He/she/they made me...

Life is difficult for me

I can't help it....

You just do not understand.

When things are going badly, not to my liking, then

someone is to blame.

It is necessary to identify the person(s), circumstance(s), or why things are not as I think they should be

Neither growth nor learning results from the awful things which happen to me.

I have just described the *Victim* mentality.

But here's another way of responding to any given event:

I unconditionally accept everything which has ever happened to me, or is currently happening to me, and will happen to me in the future because it helps me learn and grow. No one other than me can be rightly blamed for any negativity, hurts or abuses which I experience.

What you just read is fully responsible persons thinking.

It is not your boss, your spouse, your children, or any external source which causes your emotions. Your feelings are under your control, and they begin with the words you use to think about the situations and events of your life. Criticism too hinders interpersonal relationships, hinders work, and inhibits creativity; it can hurt and wound.

How can you develop awareness in order to choose?

Often there is *stimulus than reaction*

But there is also:

Stimulus then choice than reaction

The key to releasing the victim mentality is self-awareness. With practice, we can become aware of those times and situations when we enter into the victim mentality. Awareness

empowers us to turn a reaction into a
response, to change the negative into a
positive. This determines the quality of
individual expression— our character!

Let's face it, recognizing our victim behaviors
can be funny. Humor helps us step back and
have a legitimate laugh at ourselves.

9

THE PATH OF LOVE AND HEALING

Whenever we hurt, for whatever reason, some part of us—usually the childlike part cries out "Stop, or I'll die"! Then, through tears, a desire for some form of recognition and compensation takes shape. A piece of food, candy, money, whatever it may be, bring the teary, blurred world back into focus.

Death quickly fades away and life resumes.[x]

This is the way it works for children.

A *piece* of something does not heal the threat of death it only hides it.

All the *pieces* in the world we use to establish our own identities are, in the end, nothing but delusion. PTSD (post-traumatic stress disorder) is nothing but the shocking and painful awareness of what we already know but choose to hide. The trauma which has brought us just inches from death shows us with shocking clarity, all of our defenses against death are just empty illusions.

Even as adults, there will always be a childlike part of us who seeks some recognition of our pain and some compensation.

If we get caught in feelings of victimization, then, we will always be trying to tell others what to do. This can happen openly through argumentativeness, protest, or aggression and it can happen in subtle, unconscious ways, such as sarcasm, and passive aggressiveness. When others do not do what we want them to do, then we feel even more victimized. It all becomes a vicious circle.

If you look back on your life honestly, you will likely see how often you have been involved with adverse situations. We all have. This does not mean you want to suffer; it indicates people most often choose what they know over what is unknown. If you have grown up knowing abuse and humiliation, even though abuse and humiliation are not pleasant this is known and predictable, and in this sense it is comfortable.

This is *masochism*, preferring (desiring) humiliation unconsciously because it is more "comfortable" than facing the unknown with thru personal responsibility.

This is the difference between desire (unconscious) and want (conscious). You can desire what you do not even want. When a situation is not in accord, in your unconscious, you will continue to do unpleasant things. The unconscious yearning for self-punishment and shame will continue to influence you into unpleasant situations, even if consciously you do not want them at all.

What is the deepest motivation for all this unconsciously self-inflicted pain? It is the indirect hope you make yourself feel loved. What? It is the belief others in seeing how much you are willing to tolerate abuse, will

somehow be made to acknowledge you.
Then, in seeing yourself reflected in their eyes,
you will have the pleasure of feeling loved.

This hope of feeling loved brings us, finally to
the difference between humility and
masochism. To live in humility is to live
always in complete confidence of the
Universe's love, protection, and guidance,
and, therefore, to have no concerns for
yourself when others insult you—or praise
you. Secure in the Universe's love, you do
not have to base your identity on whether or
not others acknowledge you. In masochism,
on the other hand, you invite others to insult
you because, as a psychological defense
against the pain of deep emotional wounds,
you get unconscious pleasure in being
demeaned, in the secret hope, you will
somehow, someday, gain someone's

appreciation for your willingness to endure painful abuse.

You begin the process of inner healing by listening to your unconscious. Examine your dreams. Explore your pain and anger. Face up to the terror of your inner loneliness. Find strength in your weakness. Overcome your fears of losing your identity, by giving up voluntarily. With dedication and discipline, you will find the ability to give up your pride, forgive those who have hurt you, and give yourself in pure love. Then you will be on the path of life and healing.

10

PERSONAL POWER

*The meeting of two personalities is like the contact of
two substances: if there is any reaction, both are
transformed."*

-C. G. Jung

[xi]For many people, relationships are the most rewarding and sometimes the most challenging and painful of human experiences. Our first role models for relationships are usually our parents. Before you decide to blame them for your failed relationships, remember: they got their relationship "software" from their parents who got theirs from their parents, and so on. Blaming your parents or others for your relationship difficulties just reinforces the problem. When you accuse others of your problems you establish and/or reinforce a victim mentality at the subconscious level. This program says other people and forces control your life. With beliefs like this, you can see why you attract people and situations which make life difficult. The subconscious mind is simply programmed to

recognize and attract what is familiar, not necessarily what is desirable. When you list all the qualities you want in a relationship partner be sure you possess those qualities yourself in order to attract them!

Self-Esteem

Are Subconscious beliefs sabotaging your self-esteem?

Your self-esteem profoundly influences how others perceive you. If your self-esteem is high, other people will tend to see you this way. However, if your self-esteem is low, others will respond accordingly with a lack of confidence and trust in you. Essentially, your beliefs (especially the subconscious ones) are teaching the world how to treat you. The way people treat you are a reflection of subconscious beliefs. Consequently, if you want to change the way others behave toward you, you want to change the self-sabotaging beliefs which are causing the undesirable treatment. As the saying goes, "If you cannot love yourself, you cannot expect others to."

Another aspect of self-esteem is the concept of unworthiness. This subconscious programmed belief leads to a deep sense of hopelessness and helplessness. To add insult to injury, you may consciously think this should be different though subconsciously you believe you are not worthy of having it be different. If you want to be free of the limitations of unworthiness in your life, be sure your subconscious beliefs support this goal.

"Our deepest fear is not we are inadequate. Our deepest fear is we are powerful beyond measure. It is our light, not our darkness, which most frightens us. We ask ourselves, "Who am I to be brilliant, gorgeous, talented… fabulous?" Actually, who are you not to be? You are a child of God. Your playing small doesn't serve the world. There is nothing enlightened about shrinking so people won't feel insecure around you. We were born to make manifest the glory of God which is within us. It's not just in some of us; it's in everyone. And when we let our own light shine, we unconsciously give other people permission to do the same. As we are liberated from our own fear our presence automatically liberates others."

Nelson Mandel's Inaugural speech

Personal Power

Are subconscious beliefs sabotaging your personal power?

Increase your confidence and willingness to take positive and decisive action in your life. If, as a child, you heard messages from parents and other authority figures, which told you, your opinion did not matter, and your actions did not matter, you are likely to have subconscious beliefs, which mirror those, ideas. The result is often a person with strong insecurities about their ability to positively influence the course of their lives. Some people overcompensate for this feeling of powerlessness by making a career out of becoming powerful. Usually this sense of power is achieved by acquiring money, possessions and social status. Unfortunately, these external signs of power rarely satisfy the gnawing feeling of insecurity and powerlessness. People with authentic power can have a wealth of money, possessions and social status. Their personal power does not come from the things they have, but rather from who they are. Are these subconscious beliefs supporting your full potential or do you hold conflicting beliefs which are sabotaging your personal power?

Sample Beliefs:

1. I take the initiative to shape my life the way I want
2. I express my personal truths with love, passion and commitment
3. I learn from my fears as they lead me to knowledge and power
4. I am willing to take risks to live my life openly and honestly

5. I actively embrace the
    opportunities which come with
    change

Consciously renouncing the victim mentality

We are not victims of our experience. Secretly or not, we feel like victims, even those who in the world's eyes have been extremely fortunate: "Oh, I've had such a hard time." Even if, we suffered, in the present moment we decided to be free. A victim is helpless. It is a neurotic habit to take refuge in victim consciousness. A person who wants to be free rejects it and takes full responsibility for all life, all karma.

Only one person makes choices—me. I'm the
only one doer.

Our Cells & Victim Mentality

In the past, when I awoke on most mornings
my routine was to get the coffee brewing, sit
in my lounge chair and turn on CNN for the
news.

One morning, I took my coffee to my favorite
chair in the living room and turned on CNN.
The first news story I tuned in, was a mother
35, and her three children, ages 10,11, and 8,
all shot to death in their SUV in a town, forty
miles outside of Chicago. A man found shot
but with non-threatening injuries. The police
were thinking it is domestic.

The following story was about a young man who was accidentally released from a New Jersey Police station—he was in there for murdering two people! Oops—that's a mistake. Now the police search for him.

By the end, of the story, I had enough of the news. I shut off the TV and picked up the current book I was reading *"The Attractor Factor" by Joe Vitale*. My mind began drifting before I started reading. I questioned myself as to why I start my day with death and darkness watching CNN. I know better, I do not watch the evening news before I put my head down on my pillow as I fall asleep.

All this negativity cannot be a terrific way to start the day. Why was I allowing all this victim mentality into my living room?

Our cells in our bodies are literally submerged with all of this victim mentality.

11

ACCEPTING RESPONSIBILITY IN YOUR PERSONAL RELATIONSHIPS

For many of us, relationships are the most rewarding and sometimes the most challenging and painful of human experiences. Our first role models for relationships are usually our parents.

Before you decide to blame them for your failed relationships, remember: they acquired their relationship "software" from their parents, who attained theirs from their parents, and so on.[xii]

Blaming your parents or others for your relationship difficulties just reinforces the problem. When you blame others for your problems you establish and/or reinforce a victim mentality at the subconscious level. This program says other people and forces control your life. With beliefs like this you can see why you attract people and situations which make life difficult.   The subconscious mind is programmed to recognize and attract what is familiar, not necessarily what is desirable. When you list all the qualities you want in a relationship partner be sure you possess those qualities yourself in order to attract them!

I did blame my parents earlier in my life, but after receiving therapy, I learned this is the easy way. Parents are not perfect, and I know I am not a perfect parent. I learned my parents did the best they could with what they knew. Since they were both raised in dysfunctional homes, this is all they knew. It is up to each of us to recognize the dysfunction pattern and change it. I can point a finger, but three are pointing back at me. It was easy to blame decisions I had chosen which did not turn out well, on my childhood. It had to be my parents fault was my thought. This is the easy way out, blaming others for your own shortcomings and wrong decisions. Instead of blaming others when something does not go well, or the way I think it should, I look within to see where my heart and head are.

Blaming others is easy, accepting you have faults and are not perfect, and do not know everything, is big. Once you accept this, you do not make mistakes, *you are learning life lessons.*

EPILOGUE

Since I began writing this book, much change has happened in my life. My husband and I moved from a ski resort in Colorado, to the Western Slope of the state.

Five months after relocating, my husband suffered a massive heart attack and forced him to be hospitalized for a month.

During this month's time, he underwent three surgeries, including a quadruple bi-pass. The evening of the bi-pass, he went into *code blue* twelve times. I was in his ICU room several times when this occurred. Doctors, nurses rushing into the room, chaos all around me as I stood motionlessly, as I watch my husband of only four short years die before my eyes.

The following morning when I went home to get some rest, I answered one of the many awaiting e-mails in my Inbox. I replied to my friend Karen's e-mail in which she wrote *"I am in tears for what you are going through." "I'll send positive energy your way, I love you, Karen".*

My response to her was — *"Karen, thanks. If I believed in hell, this would be what I would imagine it to be. I'm pulling on every part of my being to go through this. Begging to a God, I have not had much*

faith in, in the past. I need more than four years I've
shared with Brett. They are keeping him sedated now
so his body can heal, but the doctors do not know. I
am experiencing the same gut wrenching pain I felt
when my father was ill. I'm not asking how much
more a person can take because I will just get more
shit thrown at me. I have no one here, and it is
difficult. I do my best to be strong when I update
Brett's son on the telephone. I do not want to do this
Karen, yet I do not have a choice. Thanks for your
positive thoughts and please keep them coming. Love
you more, Donna.

The following week, my husband's health was
not much better after the bi-pass surgery a
week earlier. His doctor sat me down and told
me the best chance he would have to have my
husband live was to get him back into surgery
and place a pace maker with defibrillator in.
He cautioned because of his weakened state, it

was quite possible his body would not be able to handle the surgery, and he could die on the operating table. After considerable thought, I told the doctor to move forward with the surgery. Within an hour, we were leaving his ICU unit, to surgery. The staff allowed me to walk beside his bed to the operating room. Silence in the elevator as we move down to the first floor. Once we arrived outside the surgery room doors, I am told to say my goodbyes.

I bent forward, and in-between the many IV's and machines which were keeping him alive, I kissed his cheek, and as a tear rolled down my face I said goodbye, and slowly walked to the same waiting room I waited in during his two earlier surgeries. The first surgery seemed as though it took place years before, when in actuality it had only been eight long days.

Two hours later, the doctor came out to tell me the surgery was a success, and he survived. Soon the nurse came to have me accompany them back to ICU.

Three weeks later, Brett came home from the hospital. It has been twenty-three months since his first surgery. His health is better, although his heart is only working at twenty percent, and we are told this is the best his heart will ever get, without a transplant.

I end with this story because I am living proof life throws everyone curve balls. It is critical how you cope with situations. I never considered myself a victim nor did my husband, during this time, or ever. It is life, and what we do to learn and grow through situations life presents to us, is what's necessary.

I would be lying if I said it was like a walk in the park, it was not. I continue to see the glass half full, rather than half empty.

"All blame is a waste of time. No matter how much fault you find with another, and regardless of how much you blame him, it will not change you... You may succeed in making another feel guilty of something by blaming him; you won't succeed in changing whatever it is about you that is making you unhappy."

Wayne Dyer

REFERENCES

1   APA: Eliminating Our Own Victim Mentality - EFFECTIVE ... (n.d.). Retrieved from http://hodu.com/victim.shtml.

2   APA: Articles | | San Diego Family Counseling | Lana VeytsSan ... (n.d.). Retrieved from http://www.sandiegofamilycounseling.com/?page_id=250.

3   APA: Welcome To Mary Bondi. (n.d.). Retrieved from http://www.marybondi.com/changepower.html.

4   APA: Parenting Articles about Accountability & Responsibility. (n.d.). Retrieved from http://www.empoweringparents.com/category-Accountability-And-Responsibility.php.

5   Victim Mentality Quiz | - | Consultant

idea swap, positive ... (n.d.). Retrieved from
http://mkrules.wordpress.com/2007/09/25/v
ictim-mentality/

6, 7 APA: Eliminating Our Own Victim
Mentality - EFFECTIVE ... (n.d.). Retrieved
from http://hodu.com/victim.shtml

8   APA: Why Taking Responsibility is the
MOST Important Step to Your ... (n.d.).
Retrieved from
http://community.sedona.com/letting-go-
articles/643-why-taking-responsibility-most-
important-step-your-health-well-being.html

9   APA: Knowledge Sharing: TRP - Totally
Responsible Person. (n.d.). Retrieved from
http://carpenterlibraryknowledgesharing.blog
spot.com/2009/09/trp-totally-responsible-
person.html

10 APA: The Dark Night : True Love : False
Spirituality : Being a ... (n.d.). Retrieved from
http://www.guidetopsychology.com/reltx.htm

11,12   APA: PSYCH-K Centre International | Relationships. (n.d.). Retrieved from http://psych-k.com/relationships.html

Inspirational Quotes:

I've learned that people will forget what you
said, people will forget what you did, but
people will never forget how you made them
feel.
Maya Angelou

Happiness is not something you postpone for
the future; it is something you design for the
present.
Jim Rohn

Clouds come floating into my life, no longer
to carry rain or usher storm, but to add color
to my sunset sky.
Rabindranath Tagore

Nothing is impossible; the word itself says
'I'm possible'!
Audrey Hepburn

Don't let the fear of striking out hold you
back.
Babe Ruth

Change your thoughts and you change your world.
Norman Vincent Peale

Adopting the right attitude can convert a negative stress into a positive one.
~Dr Hans Selye

Every day may not be good, but there's something good in every day.
~Unknown

A person will sometimes devote all his life to the development of one part of his body – the wishbone.
~Robert Frost

Do all the negative, self-limiting thoughts come to the forefront and stop you in your tracks? You must learn to change these self-imposed limitations that are preventing you from reaching your potential.
~Anita Foley

If you don't like the road you're walking, pave another one.
~Dolly Parton

Self-pity in its early stages is as snug as a
feather mattress. Only when it hardens does it
become uncomfortable.
Maya Angelou

DONNA LIVELY

ABOUT THE AUTHOR

Donna, born and raised in a small town, south
of Cleveland, Ohio, is the third of six
daughters of Herbert and Marilyn Humm. In
2006, after living single since her divorce nine
years earlier, she moved to Northern
California. Later the same year, she relocated
to Fraser, Colorado where she married her
seventh grade sweetheart. Since childhood,
she has written poems, fiction and non-fiction
stories, newspaper stories, and company
newsletters. She currently lives on the
Western Slope of Colorado with her husband
Brett.

DONNA LIVELY

Made in the USA
San Bernardino, CA
05 April 2013